FIRST GUIDE
TO CIVIL WAR
GENEALOGY AND RESEARCH

Third Edition

By Gerald Post

Order this book online at www.trafford.com
or email orders@trafford.com

Most Trafford titles are also available at major online book retailers.

Note for Librarians: A cataloguing record for this book is available from Library
and Archives Canada at www.collectionscanada.ca/amicus/index-e.html

Printed in Victoria, BC, Canada.

ISBN: 978-1-4269-2048-6

*Our mission is to efficiently provide the world's finest, most comprehensive book publishing
service, enabling every author to experience success. To find out how to publish your
book, your way, and have it available worldwide, visit us online at www.trafford.com*

Trafford rev. 1/22/09

 www.trafford.com

North America & international
toll-free: 1 888 232 4444 (USA & Canada)
phone: 250 383 6864 ♦ fax: 812 355 4082

Table of Contents

"The past rises before me like a dream, again we are in the struggle for national life."

G. W. Bailey

About the Author

Gerald Post became interested the Civil War after inheriting his great grandfather's Civil War diary which he published, *The Civil War Diary and Biography of George W. Bailey*. Gerald is a Civil War re-enactor with an Artillery Unit and appeared in the movie Gettysburg. He graduated from Western Michigan University, has an Electrical Engineering Certificate from Michigan State University and a MBA from Western Connecticut University.

Chapter 1

Introduction

The years 2011 through 2015 mark the Sesquicentennial (150th) Anniversary of the great American Civil War. This historic event will generate a renewed interest in "all things Civil War" and now is a good time to research and learn about your Civil War ancestors.

If any of your ancestors were living in America at the time of the Civil War, chances are very good that your great or great-great-grandfather (you have eight of them) was one of the 3.5 million soldiers who fought for either the North or South.

If this is the case, the good news is that there probably is a wealth of information about your Civil War Confederate or Union ancestor and his military unit waiting for you in some dusty archive. And, getting your own copy of these records is as easy as going online to the Web sites listed in this book.

About this book

This book gives you the information needed for your own Confederate or Union Civil War genealogical research. Chapter 2 provides a "Quick Start" method using the Internet to get you started on your research with a minimum effort. The remainder of this book:

First Guide to Civil War Genealogy

- Explains how and where (Web sites and addresses are provided) to get information about your ancestors from the National Archives, State Archives, the census records, the Internet, local libraries and many other sources.
- Provides ways to analyze the information. Since most readers are interested in either a Union or Confederate ancestor, chapters are arranged so that you can zero in on the source of information for either your Johnny Reb or Billy Yank ancestor.
- Provides background information on the Civil War that is useful in understanding the nature of the various Civil War records.
- Relates the author's own experience searching the various records and describes the information he was able to obtain about his own Civil War ancestor.
- Describes the new computerized Civil War Soldiers and Sailors System (CWSS). This online database can be used to access individual information of over 3 million soldiers and sailors using records at the National Archives.
- Provides an extensive list of resource material including Internet locations.

Civil War Genealogical Research

It has been said that genealogy and history cannot be separated and Civil War genealogy is certainly a case in point. Genealogy is defined as a branch of history that involves the determination of family relationships. Civil War genealogy then is the search for that individual and any family information in Civil War military records and related sources. Once the researcher has found the basic records related to a soldier, he or she can begin to recreate an ancestor's military career, following him through the battles and the day to day life of a Civil War soldier.

The simplest way to start your genealogical research is with yourself and your parents. Fill in an Ancestor Chart (free on many Web sites, see Chapter 2) with whatever information you have. Then check with family members, especially grandparents, to see if they can fill in any more lines on the Ancestor Chart. Hopefully, this will lead you back to the name and information on your Civil War ancestor. Once you have found his name you can begin the search for his military records and learn about his experiences in the Civil War.

The primary sources for this information are the service and pension records. Information from these records can be fleshed out using secondary sources such as medical records, prisoner of war records and regimental histories. Finally all of this information must be summarized in a form usable to others. This summary is the gift, if not the obligation, that the researcher has to current and future generations. The summary might take the form of standard genealogical reports such as a pedigree chart, descendant's chart, or in a narrative form such as a book or paper. Today's technology allows us to record and disseminate genealogical information as never before. Dozens of genealogy computer programs are now available to record and summarize the information and to print charts and reports. The Internet is a ubiquitous tool that allows genealogical researchers to share resources on a worldwide basis.

When doing Civil War research, it is important to set goals and to stay focused on these goals. Simply stated, these goals should be:

1. Obtain copies of the service and pension records using the "Quick Start" described in Chapter 2.
2. Obtain a history of his regiment and study the battles and campaigns in which he fought.
3. Obtain any additional information such as medical records, prisoner records, amnesty records and burial records.
4. Collect and assemble "standard genealogical data" such as family relationships plus birth, marriage and death dates using sources such as census records, probate records, land records, family histories, etc. The Bibliography lists several good genealogy books that can help you in this process.

5. The fifth goal is to record all of this information in a usable form and to share it with others. This is where computer programs for genealogy are especially helpful.

Along the way to achieving these goals, it is important to keep good notes and to document your findings. Some kind of filing system is also a necessity, whether it is file folders in a cabinet or shoe boxes marked with a felt tip pen. It is amazing how fast papers, notes and reports can pile up once you start a genealogy project!

Chapter 2

"Quick Start" to Obtaining Civil War Records
Using the Internet

Follow these three steps:

Step 1: Was your ancestor in the Civil War?
Step 2: Order his records from the National Archives
Step 3: Discover his regimental history and battles

Step 1: Was Your Ancestor in the Civil War?

The first thing to do is to discover if your ancestor was actually in the Civil War and if his records exist at the National Archives. Go online and access the *Civil War Soldiers and Sailors System* (CWSS) at **www.itd.nps.gov/cwss**. The system is self explanatory and very easy to use: Select "Soldiers" and enter as much information as you have including last name, first name, Union or Confederate, state of origin, military unit, and function such as infantry, cavalry, sharpshooter or engineer. You don't have to enter all of this information to get some results, just start with whatever information you can find.

The CWSS database contains basic information on 6.3 million soldier names so that if your ancestor was in the Civil War, chances are that his name will be listed. If successful, your search will be rewarded with his rank(s), regiment(s) and company (ies). The CWSS also includes histories of over 4,000 regiments with rosters, both Union and Confederate. So, knowing which regiment he served in, you can make an educated guess as to which battles he was in. A word of caution however, the fact that he was in a certain regiment, e.g. Michigan 3rd, should not be used as proof that he actually fought at a specific battle such as the Battle of Gettysburg.

Assuming you know his name and whether Confederate or Union, you may not know his state or unit. For this Quick Start effort, draw the information from family records, old letters, diaries, local histories, a visit to your local library or make an educated guess at his home state and unit, enter it in the CWSS online form and hope for the best. If you have no clues as to service branch, keep in mind that the vast majority of men were in the volunteer army infantry. Unfortunately, only a portion of the Union and Confederate sailors are now included in the CWSS. Likewise, the CWSS does not include records for those in the Regular Army. See Chapter 7 for ways to search for these records. More information on the CWSS is provided in Chapter 10.

Step 2: Ordering Records from the National Archives

Now that you have verified that your ancestor was in the Civil War using the CWSS, the next step is to order copies of his records from the National Archives. When ordered online, you will receive an Email confirming your request and be able to track your order online. The primary records available at the National Archives, the Compiled Military Service Records and the Pension Records, are discussed as follows:

Compiled Military Service Records (CMSR)

A compiled service record is an abstract (not the actual record itself) of a soldier's military record and consists of a card or cards on which his service information was recorded. The Union and Confederate service records were compiled by the War Department several years after the Civil War to allow a more rapid means to verify claims for pensions that amounted to more than $5 billion by 1930. In this massive project all available documents were reviewed and abstracts for each soldier were placed in a jacket (folder) bearing his name, rank and military unit. There is one CMSR for each regiment in which he served. The jackets containing the compiled service records are arranged by state, by military unit and then alphabetically by surname. The compiled service records were created to verify military service and contain little if any genealogical information. They do, however, usually list his rank, unit, whether he was present at roll calls, pay, facts of enlistment and discharge, any wounds or hospitalization and if he was a prisoner of war. Confederate CMSRs are also available at the National Archives but are not as extensive as the Union records. Refer to Chapter 7 for detailed information on the CMSRs.

Army Volunteer CMSRs may be ordered on the Internet at **www.eservices.archives.gov/orderonline** using NATF Form 86. The cost is $25 (includes shipping and handling) and may be charged using a major credit card. Your choice of either paper copies or a CD/DVD will ship in four to six weeks. There is no charge for an unsuccessful search.

The minimum required information is 1) Veteran's full name, 2) State which he served, 3) Union or Confederate, and 4) Volunteer or Regular. Additional information such as his regiment is usually required for a successful search as discussed in the Tips section below.

Pension Records

Pension records generally include much more information of interest to the genealogical researcher, i.e., birth date and place, wife's name, marriage date and place, where lived, children's names and ages, etc. Often, an applicant had to document his military service to qualify for a pension and you may find supporting letters written by him, his fellow soldiers and his family. Sometimes pages from the family Bible were submitted to prove a marriage. All these papers are still in the National Archives and can be a gold mine of information as shown by the author's experience see Chapter 4.

Union pension records may be ordered at **www.eservices. archives.gov/orderonline** using NATF Form 85. The cost is $75 (includes shipping and handling) for the first 100 pages and may be charged using a major credit card. If the file exceeds 100 pages, you will get a form with instructions. Your choice of either paper copies or a CD/DVD will ship in four to six weeks. There is no charge for an unsuccessful search.

The minimum required information is 1) Veteran's full name, 2) State which he served, 3), army, navy or marines, and 4) Volunteer or Regular. Additional information such as regiment is usually required for a successful search.

Confederate pension records are not kept at the National Archives since the Federal Government did not give pensions to Confederate veterans. Confederate pension records are only available from individual states that gave pensions to their veterans and widows. Initially, the Southern states only granted pensions to the wounded but eventually they gave pensions to all qualified veterans and their widows. Eligibility for a state pension was based on the state of residency at the time of application, not where he enlisted or served. Chapter 8 explains how you can obtain Confederate pensions records from the state archives.

Tips for Completing NATF Forms 85 and 86

Unless your ancestor had a very unusual name, it is unlikely that the staff will be able to find him without additional information. There may be dozens of men named "John A. Smith" in the New York State records and the overworked clerk at the National Archives has no way of knowing which John A. Smith is yours. Your chances of getting a response will be vastly improved if you include the name of the unit in which he served, e.g., the 157th New York Infantry, Terry's Texas Rangers, etc. Chapter 7 provides methods for finding his unit. If you have any other information about your ancestor such as duty stations and dates, birth date, hometown, etc., be sure to include it.

If the staff at the National Archives responds that they cannot find any records for your ancestor, then refer to

Chapters 7 and 8 for help finding the correct state, service branch and unit. You can then resubmit the NATF form with the updated information.

If he was in more than one regiment, a separate NATF form must be submitted for each set of records. For example, if he was in the 3rd Regiment but was later transferred to the 5th regiment, two forms must be sent in to get all of his service records.

The NARA does not have records on veterans in state militia units, the equivalent of today's National Guard. These records will be found in the State Archives, see Chapter 8. Likewise the NARA does not yet have CMSRs for men who served in the Navy, Marine Corps or the Regular Army. Refer to Chapter 7 for sources for these records.

Step 3: Discover His Regimental History and Battles

For a Quick Start introduction to your ancestor's regimental history, access the *Civil War Soldiers and Sailors System* (CWSS) at **www.itd.nps.gov/cwss**. Click on Regiments and enter the basic information requested on the form. You will be rewarded with a one page summary of the regiment's history and links to major battles in which it fought. Keep in mind that this is not proof that your ancestor actually fought in that battle, he may have been on sick call, special duty, etc.

"Quick Start" is Only the Beginning

If you find information on your Civil War ancestor as the result of this Quick Start, congratulations! If not, do not be discouraged, try using the research methods suggested in this book to find his military unit or other information that will direct the archivist at the NARA to his records. Or, some people have had success just by sending in a new NATF Form with the same information, maybe the staff at the Archives had a bad day when going through the records for the first time.
Chapter 2 lists several Web sites besides the CWSS which may provide valuable clues to finding your Civil War ancestors and his records. Some sites allow you to view individual

records online and to print copies (for a fee).

If you need the information in a hurry and have the money to spend, a professional researcher can usually get the copies for you in two or three weeks. Better yet, make a vacation trip of it, go to the National Archives in Washington and make the copies yourself. Check the National Archives Web site for procedures for a personal visit.

This "Quick Start" is only the beginning; do not stop your research at this point. The next step is to get a more detailed history of his military unit and to see if there is any information about your ancestor in the state archives. If your ancestor was a Confederate, write to the state archives for his pension records. In addition, there may be a wealth of information available from other sources as discussed in the following chapters. You may get lucky as I did and find a plethora of fascinating data on your ancestor, including some heroic actions or maybe a forgotten scandal in the family tree.

Chapter 3

Internet Civil War Sites

Web sites come and go; the following list was verified at the time this book was published. There may be a charge for some of these sites. The Web sites are continuously updating and adding digitized databases which can greatly enhance your ability to search the records from the National and State Archives. Check out these sites on a routine basis for the latest updates.

American Civil War Research Database
www.civilwardata.com

Has state rosters, regimental histories, pension indexes and may be used to find a soldier's regiment. "Historical Data Systems has created the only database of its kind that can be used for statistical and analytical examinations of the War. It is now possible to examine and measure the impact these individual soldier experiences had upon regimental effectiveness."

Ancestry Magazine
www.ancestry.com/search

Has several databases including one similar to the CWSS. Also, Civil War POW records, colored troops military records and the complete U.S. Census. Databases containing more than 16 million names and thousands of government records available to search and print. Where available, names are linked to several databases so that one entry yields a "life view" of the soldier.

Civil War.Com
www.civilwar.com

Includes links to interactive histories of over 300 CW battles with photos. Several searchable databases. Also includes the entire Civil War Official Record (OR). List of Civil War Round Tables searchable by state and city, reenactments and discussion groups.

Civil War Archives: United States Colored Troops
www.civilwararchive.com/unioncol.htm

Listing and history of all Union regiments with colored troops

Civil War Preservation Trust
www.civilwar.org/

The mission of the CWPT is to protect and preserve battlefields threatened by modern developments. Has listing of battlefields, events and a center for teachers and students.

Civil War Rosters Arranged by State
www.geocities.com/area51/lair/3680/cw/cw.html

Civil War Soldiers and Sailors System (CWSS)
www.itd.nps.gov/cwss

Refer to Chapter 10. "A computerized database containing very basic facts about servicemen who served on both sides during the Civil War. The initial focus of the CWSS is the *Names Index Project*, a project to enter names and other basic information from 6.3 million soldier records in the National Archives. The facts about the soldiers were entered from records that are indexed to many millions of other documents about Union and Confederate Civil War soldiers.

Confederate Research Center
http://www.hillcollege.edu/museum/

A major center for Confederate research located in Hill College, Hillsboro, Texas.

Cyndi's List: US Civil War
www. cyndislist.com/cw.htm

The mother lode for all Web sites relating to the Civil War

Daughters of Union Veterans of the Civil War
www.duvcw.org

Has history and records of the organization, activities, etc.

Department of Veterans Affairs National Gravesite Locator
www.gravelocator.cem.va.gov
Search for burial locations of veterans and their family members in VA National Cemeteries, state veterans cemeteries, various other military and Department of Interior cemeteries, and for veterans buried in private cemeteries when the grave is marked with a government grave marker. Includes information on both national and state cemeteries

Family History Library
www.familysearch.org

Operated by the Mormon Church. Has extensive genealogical as well as Civil War related databases with search and print capability. Also has lots of "getting started" help and a free genealogy program.

Family Tree Maker Magazine
www.familytreemagazine.com

Has several articles on genealogy and searching for Civil War ancestors. Also provides free genealogical forms, research tools, "getting started help", blogs, etc. Also has reviews of genealogy programs and Web sites.

Footnote
www.footnote.com

Has partnered with National Archives to digitize images of microfilmed Civil War records including compiled service records, pension files, etc. Search and print available

Grand Army of the Republic
www. suvcw.org/research.htm

Sons of Union Veterans of the Civil War, links to articles and history of the GAR

Helm's Genealogy Toolbox
www.genealogytoolbox.com

"The Genealogy Toolbox is collection of tools to assist in researching genealogy or family history. Provides links to hundreds of Civil War Web sites with content relevant to family history resources."

National Archives and Records Administration
www.archives.gov/research/civil-war/
www.archives.gov/genealogy/military/
www.archives.gov/genealogy/census
www.archives.gov/genealogystart-research

Starting points for information about civil war, genealogy, military and census records held at the National Archives

National Park Service Civil War Homepage
www.nps.gov/civilwar

An excellent place to start and expand your Civil War research. List of Civil War related National Parks, schedule of events, Civil War flags, etc.

Sons of Confederate Veterans
www.scv.org

Grave registry, genealogical assistance, reenactments, event calendar, etc.

Sons of Union Veterans of the Civil War
www.suvcw.org/home

Provides membership information, activities, organization history. Maintains a National Graves Registration Database

Chapter 4

Some Personal Experiences Using Civil War Records

A few years ago I inherited the Civil War diary of my great-grandfather, George W. Bailey. He was from Allegan, Michigan and served in the 3rd Michigan Infantry from June 1861 until he was discharged in April 1865.

Reading the diary for the first time, I was fascinated with his experiences in all the battles from First Bull Run in 1861 through the Battle of the Wilderness in April 1864 where he was captured and sent to Andersonville Prison in Georgia. What kind of man was he that he could survive all of this and yet return to his home after the war and raise a family of 10 children? The answer to this question led me to a research project involving the National Archives, state archives, trips to libraries and museums, visits to National Parks at Gettysburg and Andersonville, correspondence with dozens of his descendants and finally to an interest in Civil War reenacting. The trail also led me into the field of genealogy where I was able to trace his lineage back to the 1600's in France and to track down 214 of his descendants.

As the diary had never been published, I decided to share the results of my Civil War and genealogical research by publishing the results in a book entitled, *The Civil War Diary and Biography of George W Bailey.* This new book, *First*

Guide, was written to share some of the tools you can use for your own Civil War research.

The National Archives proved to be a treasure chest of information on Private George Bailey and most of it came to me by simply going on the Internet as described in the "Quick Start" in Chapter 2. One surprising bit of information that turned up in his service records was that George Bailey was twice charged with desertion! First, when he was captured at the Battle of The Wilderness, his officers thought he had been killed or deserted. However, when they later discovered he had been taken prisoner and sent to Andersonville Prison, the records show that he was reinstated and his status changed to "captured in battle." Later, when he was released from Andersonville Prison in 1865 too sick to serve, he was sent home on furlough to rest, yet somehow his papers were mixed up and they thought he had deserted from furlough. Copies of letters obtained from the National Archives show that Bailey wrote from his home in Michigan to Washington asking why he had not received orders to appear for discharge. Somehow the matter was cleared up and he was given an honorable discharge from service on April 14, 1865.

The service records also listed his clothing and equipment issues as well as his pay, which was usually late, his duty status, and whether he was present for muster, on sick call or off on special duty.

The pension records revealed a possible scandal in the family tree! When George Bailey died in 1905, his widow and the mother of his ten children filed for a widow's pension. Copies of the correspondence obtained from the National Archives show that when the clerk in Washington tried to verify the marriage of Mary and George Bailey with the clerk at the Allegan County Court House, no record of the marriage could be found. This must have been a great shock to Mary and her ten children! However, it is good news to his descendant's generations later because it created a flurry of correspondence as Mary's friends and family wrote letters to Washington testifying that she and George were indeed married. All these letters are in the National Archives pension files and they reveal much about the Bailey family and life in the 1800's that had been lost to their descendants. (Yes, they were able to prove the marriage and Mary received her widow's pension.)

The National Archives was also a source of information on the history of George Bailey's unit, The 3rd Michigan Infantry. A summary of the regimental history was available online. Copies of the original documents of the 3rd are available on microfilm from the National Archives and make fascinating reading. A search of the state archives produced an even more detailed history of his unit while the state library produced further information in an 1882 book, *Michigan in the War.* For example, the records show that the 3rd Infantry fought in 49 separate engagements from First Bull Run in July 1861 to the Battle of Cold Harbor in June 1864. In July 1863, the 3rd fought in the Peach Orchard in Gettysburg and the following day they were on the receiving end of Pickett's Charge.

The records also show that after the Battle of Gettysburg the 3rd was sent by steamer to New York City to help quell the draft riots that threatened to undermine Lincoln's war efforts. In August, the "old veterans" as they were then called, were sent up the Hudson River to Troy, New York to inspire recruiting efforts for replacements to help fight the nation's bloodiest war. In his diary, George tells about meeting Annie Etheridge while at Troy. She served as a nurse and was called "The Daughter of the Regiment." Annie was given a battlefield promotion to sergeant for her bravery when she picked up the rifle of a fallen soldier she was nursing and continued his fight. In 1877, a thankful Congress gave her a special pension of $25 per month. George had an autographed photo of Annie tucked away in the back of his diary.

In September 1863, they traveled by steamer back down to Virginia in time to fight in the Bristoe Champaign. By the time the original 3rd Michigan was reorganized, 249 men had been killed in battle or died of disease. The reorganized 3rd fought in Tennessee and was finally mustered out of service in southern Texas in May 1866 where they had been sent to forestall a rumored invasion from Mexico

The above summary is just an example of the information available for nearly 4,000 Union and Confederate units. It makes fascinating reading, especially when you know that your own ancestor was involved.

The message of this book is that if you have a Confederate or Union ancestor who served in the Civil War, it is likely that there is a wealth of information just waiting for you. Happy hunting and I hope you will be as lucky as I was.

Chapter 5

How Civil War Units Were Raised and Organized

In March 1861, Abraham Lincoln was inaugurated President of the United States and on April 13 of that year the Confederates fired on and captured Fort Sumter in South Carolina. The United States was no longer a nation united and each side rushed to build its armies. By the end of May 1861, eleven states had seceded from the Union to form the Confederate States of America: Alabama, Arkansas, Florida, Georgia, Louisiana, Mississippi, North Carolina, South Carolina, Tennessee, Texas and Virginia. Kentucky and Missouri were not in the Confederacy but were considered as "border states" and even had provisional Confederate state governments besides their Yankee governments. The Confederacy recognized these Southern sympathizers and added a star for Kentucky and Missouri on their new flag. The Union, however, did not take kindly to this action and after some skirmishes, these two states remained in the Union. The states of Maryland and West Virginia contributed many soldiers to the Confederacy but did not formally secede. Arizona Territory was in the Confederacy for a short time at the beginning of the war but was soon placed under Union military control.

Twenty-four states remained in the Union. Two additional Union states were admitted during the war, Nevada and the State of West Virginia which was carved out of Virginia.

Whether Union or Confederate, each state hurried to raise forces to protect its home borders and to supply troops to the central governments in either Washington or Richmond. In all, approximately three million men were organized into some 4,000 Union and Confederate regiments that fought in more than 500 battles and 10,000 engagements during the four years of the Civil War. In many ways the methods used by the North and South to raise and organize the armies were the same, and yet there were many differences reflecting the background and personalities of the leaders involved.

When researching Union or Confederate unit histories, keep in mind that the Federals usually named battles after the nearest waterway while the Confederates named them after the nearest land location. For example, the Battle of Bull Run (a river) and the Battle of Manassas (a town) are the same battle. Both sides, however, referred to the largest battle of the Civil War by the same name: Gettysburg.

Union Forces

At the start of the war there were only 16,367 officers and enlisted men in the Regular Army. In April 1861 Lincoln, realizing that he would lose many of these regulars to the Southern cause called on the states for 75,000 volunteer soldiers to suppress the rebellion. A great wave of patriotism soon rolled over the Northern states and the "Sons of Abraham" rushed to be among the first to answer the call. The states responded by activating the militia and by raising regiments for the Union army. In many Northern states over half the male population between the ages of 20 and 40 went off to war. In the first few months there were so many volunteers that the army had to place a hold on accepting the new regiments organized by the states.

There is no exact information as to the number of Union men under arms but estimates range from 1.75 to 2.25 million. At first, men were mustered in for 90 days or six months. As the war settled in, enlistment periods were more often specified as three years or "until the end of the war." In March 1863, as the horrors of war became a reality, the Union government had to follow the example of the Confederacy and enacted draft laws to fill out the army. The Union granted an exemption for those who paid $300 but this was limited to conscientious objectors. As the war dragged on the Federal Government sought to increase the number of volunteers by offering them a bounty which often amounted $1,000 in some states.

Most of the units were made up of men from the same town or part of the state. They did not go off to war alone but usually joined up with their friends and neighbors. Some historians think it was this peer pressure that resulted in such high casualties as men marched shoulder to shoulder with their friends and neighbors into deadly rifle and cannon fire. No one wanted a report going home saying that he had run in the face of the enemy. After he was mortally wounded at the Battle of Gettysburg, Isaac Avery of the 6th North Carolina Regiment was reported to have said, "Tell my father I died with my face to the enemy."

The Federal army was a diverse group that included about 200,000 blacks organized into 166 black regiments. In 1996, a monument in Washington, D.C. was dedicated to honor the blacks who served in the Civil War. There was also one full brigade of American Indians. Estimates are that ten percent the Union men were foreigners, mostly from Germany and Ireland. And yes, it is well documented that more than 400 women served in the Union armies masquerading as men. In addition, there were thousands of women who served as nurses. One of the more famous was Annie Etheridge from Michigan. She served as a nurse and was called "The Daughter of the Regiment." Annie was given a battlefield promotion to sergeant for her bravery when she picked up the rifle of a fallen soldier she was nursing and continued his fight. In 1877, a thankful Congress gave her a special pension of $25 per month.

When the Union military organizations were viewed from the top down, there were armies, corps, divisions, brigades, regiments or batteries, and finally companies. Armies were designated by locality such as the Army of the Potomac. Each corps usually consisted of three divisions. Divisions normally had three brigades that in turn were composed of four or five regiments with ten companies each. The regiment was the basic unit of the infantry and cavalry, while the battery was the basic unit of the artillery. A regiment was supposed to number about one thousand men but seldom had even half that number.

Regiments were first known by unique names such as Price's Regiment, The Grand Rapids Volunteers, etc. However, when the unit was mustered into Union service, it was given an official designation structured as the number of the regiment, the state and finally the branch of service, e.g., The 3rd Michigan Volunteer Infantry, The 2nd Ohio Light Artillery. In a few cases they retained the original name. Most Civil War personnel records in the National Archives are filed under the unit designation so it is important to know your man's unit when ordering and researching the records.

The Federal regiments were organized with about 1,000 men. According to US Army regulations, a volunteer infantry regiment at full strength consisted of ten companies, each with 97 men and three officers. Each company had 1 captain, 1 first lieutenant, 1 second lieutenant, 1 first sergeant, 3 sergeants, 8 corporals, 2 musicians, 1 wagoner and 82 privates. The regiment was commanded by a colonel assisted by a lieutenant colonel, major, adjutant, quartermaster, surgeon, assistant surgeon and a hospital steward. Union regiments seldom remained at full strength. For example, in the spring of 1863 the average regiment could only muster 425 effectives. The North usually allowed its volunteer regiments to dwindle away until they were down to about 200 men. They then were broken up and the men reassigned to another unit. This demoralizing system was perpetuated by the governors of the Northern states to allow them to appoint more officers as a form of patronage. In 1861, a Private received $13.00 per month while a Brigadier General received $315.00 per month.

Confederate Forces

Exact figures are not known, but it is estimated that between 600,000 and one million men served in the Confederate Army and Navy between 1861 and 1865. As individual Southern states voted to secede, they authorized the governor to create volunteer military units. The Confederate government in Richmond also raised some units directly but most were accepted from those raised by the states. Men in units raised by the Confederacy served for three years or "until the end of the war," while men in units raised by the states were required to serve for only 12 months. Privates were paid $11 per month until 1864 when the pay was raised to $18. When the first round of 12 month enlistments started to expire in April 1862, the Confederacy was forced to enact the nation's first conscription laws. Initially, government employees, ministers as well as owners or overseers with 20 or more slaves were exempt from the draft. As in the North, a man could pay for a substitute if he had the money and did not want to serve. Initially, the age limit for serving in the military was from 18 to 35 but as the South faced severe manpower shortages in 1864, this was extended to 17 through 50 years of age. The Confederacy did not actually use blacks in combat but did have three full brigades of American Indians that fought in several battles.

Confederate military units were organized much the same as the Union which is not surprising since many Southern military leaders were trained in the North before the war, many at West Point.

The Confederate forces were organized into armies, such as The Army of Northern Virginia, then corps, then brigades and finally into regiments of infantry or cavalry, and batteries of artillery. As in the North, the basic unit was the regiment. Unlike the Union, however, the Confederacy tried not to let the units dissipate but kept the regiments alive by adding men to replace fatalities, desertions and wounded. Historians think this was a better strategy since the regimental *esprit de corps* was much higher. As in the Union army most Confederate units were first identified by a number, state, and then the branch of service such as the 10th Texas Infantry. It was common for Southern units to retain the less formal designation; the 10th Texas was also called Nelson's Infantry after its commanding officer.

Chapter 6

Overview of Available Civil War Records

This Chapter provides an overview of the Civil War records, i.e., types of records, how and where they originated and where they are maintained today. Chapters 7, 8 and 9 give the details of the records at the National Archives, state archives and those available from other sources.

The Civil War lasted more than four years and produced a legacy involving a huge quantity of records. Some historians say that today's governmental bureaucracy got its beginning in the paper mill of the Civil War. Most of these original records are located in the National Archives in Washington, D.C., state archives, historical societies, museums, universities and county court houses. Many of these records, especially those at the National Archives, have been microfilmed and copies are readily available at the National Archives and its branch offices, genealogical libraries and on the Internet.

In searching Civil War records, it helps to understand that upwards of ninety percent of the men fighting on both sides of the Civil War were in the volunteer army with the remainder being in the regular army, navy, marines or state militia. The volunteers were motivated by patriotism (or the draft), while the regulars were professional military men. The records are generally structured around the following service branches: Volunteer Union Army, Volunteer Union Navy, Regular Union

Army, Regular Union Navy and Marines, Confederate Army, Confederate Navy and Confederate Marines. Many states had their own militia that was the equivalent of today's National Guard. These units were raised by the states primarily for the defense of the state borders although many saw service in other states. Since the militia was never attached to the Federal or Confederate troops, their records are only available from the state archives.

For the purposes of this book, Civil War records have been classified as either primary or secondary:

1. Primary Records include the service records and pension records.

2. Secondary Records include all other records such as prison, medical, court martial and regimental histories.

1. Primary Records

Service Records

Service records are the first place to start your Civil War research. These records include pay vouches, muster rolls, returns, etc. The service records generally include the man's name, rank, military unit, date and place of entry into service, muster rolls, promotions, POW and hospital notations, promotions and separation either by discharge, desertion or death. In a few cases, especially if he was an officer, there will be information about his occupation, family, heirs and circumstances of death. If a man reenlisted or was reassigned to a different unit, this information will also be in his service record. These service records were summarized (compiled) for nearly all Federal and Confederate volunteer soldiers.

A compiled service record is an abstract of a soldier's military record and consists of a card or cards on which the above service information is recorded. The service records were compiled by the War Department several years after the Civil War to allow a more rapid means to verify claims for pensions that amounted to more than $5 billion by 1930. In this massive project all available documents were reviewed and abstracts for each soldier were placed in a jacket (folder) bearing his name, rank and military unit. The jackets containing the compiled service records were then arranged by state, by military unit and then alphabetically by surname. The compiled service records were created to verify military service and contain little if any genealogical information.

Union service records and the original compiled service records are only available at the National Archives in Washington. Unfortunately, there is no comprehensive name index to the records for all the Union volunteers. However, there are name indexes by state and these have been microfilmed. The compiled Union service records were not microfilmed. The service records for the Regular Union Army (22,000 men in 1865), Navy and Marines (101,000 men in 1865) were never compiled and therefore it takes more digging to get information on the men in these branches. See Chapter 7 for more details on Union service records.

Confederate service records and the original compiled service records are only available at the National Archives in Washington, D.C. As you might suspect, the records for Confederates are not as extensive as for the Union forces. Nearly all of the available Confederate service records have been compiled and are available on microfilm. Unlike the Union records, there is an "all name Index" which has been microfilmed and is available on the Internet. Service records for Confederate Naval and Marines are also available on microfilm. Refer to Chapter 7 for more details on Confederate service records.

How the National Archives came to have these Confederate records is an interesting story. After General Lee's surrender at Appomattox in April 1865, the Confederate Inspector General took all available records (many had been either intentionally or unintentionally destroyed) to Charlotte, North Carolina. The records were voluntarily turned over to the Union Government and taken to Washington, D.C. for storage. In 1903, the War Department began a project to organize the mass of

Confederate papers. In addition, each of the Southern states was asked to send all additional papers to Washington where they were copied and then returned.

The activity centered on an attempt to create a service record for each Confederate soldier and sailor. Each document was examined and an abstract card prepared for each name found in the document. The rank and unit were also entered on the card. If the document contained only one name, the abstract and the document were placed together in a jacket (folder). After all of the documents had been reviewed, the cards for each man were placed in a jacket that was filed in one of three groups, 1) units associated with a particular state, 2) units raised by the C.S.A. Government, or 3) units above regimental level or in special organizations. The project was completed in 1927 and the jackets were retained at the War Department.

In 1940, the National Archives acquired the War Department's collection of both Union and Confederate records and indexes. The first effort was to microfilm all of the records, however, they only completed the Confederate service records and Southern states that supplied men to the Union before the project was canceled by pressures from World War II. This explains why the Confederate service records are on microfilm and the Union records for the Northern states are not.

Copies of both Confederate and Union service records may be obtained from the National Archives using NATF Form 86 as discussed in Chapter 2.

Pension Records

Pension records generally include much more information of interest to the genealogical researcher, i.e., birth date and place, wife's name, marriage date and place, address and children's names and ages. The applicant had to document his military service to qualify for a pension and you may find supporting letters written by him, his fellow soldiers and his family. Sometimes pages from the family Bible were submitted to prove a marriage. All these papers are still in the National

Archives and can be a gold mine of information as shown by the author's experience. See Chapter 4.

Union pensions are stored at the National Archives in Washington DC. According to the Pension Act of 21 July 1861, the first pensions were only based on disability for persons disabled since March 4, 1861. It was not until June1890 that the first service related pensions were also awarded. Veterans had to have served at least 90 days, be honorably discharged and have a permanent disability. Their widows and children were also eligible for pensions. The pension acts of 1889 and 1915 required information about the veteran's families such as date of birth for children still living at home, wife's name, date and place of marriage plus where proof of marriage could be found. The original Union pension records are only available at the National Archives in Washington, D.C. Copies may be obtained by using NATF Form 85 as discussed in Chapter 2.

Confederate pension records are not kept at the National Archives since the Federal Government did not give pensions to Confederate veterans. Confederate pension records are only available from individual states that gave pensions to their veterans and widows. Initially, the Southern states only granted pensions to the wounded but eventually they gave pensions to all qualified veterans and their widows. Eligibility for a state pension was based on the state of residency at the time of application, not where he enlisted or served. For example, a veteran who had served with units from Georgia but lived in Arkansas at the time the pension laws were enacted was eligible to apply for a pension from Arkansas. If that same veteran served in an Arkansas regiment but moved to North Carolina after the war, then he would apply for a pension from North Carolina rather than Arkansas. Eligibility and amounts varied between the Confederate states. Alabama, for example, established a Pension Commission in 1867 which provided funds for artificial arms or legs to replace those limbs lost in battle. By 1891 the laws had been expanded to provide financial assistance for the veteran or his widow. Applicants had to prove desertion-free service with the Confederate forces, had to be indigent and could not own property valued at more than $2,000. Texas, however, set aside 1,280 acres of land in 1881 to be given to veterans or widows of veterans who were permanently disabled in the service of the Confederacy or the State of Texas. In 1889 the Texas law was changed to provide cash awards to veterans or their widow. Chapter 8 explains how and where you can obtain Confederate pensions records from the state archives.

2. Secondary Records

There are literally tons of secondary records in the National Archives, state archives, museums, libraries, historical societies, etc. Examples are: medical records, battle plans and reports, prisoner-of-war records, ship records, court martial records, diaries, unit histories, etc. One of the most useful for researching unit histories is the *Official Records of the Union and Confederate Armies in the War of the Rebellion*, often referred to as the Official Records or the OR. First printed by the government in 1900 it has 138,000 pages in 128 volumes. The OR is available at larger libraries and on the Internet. Other useful secondary records are listed in Chapter 7 National Archives, Chapter 8 - State Archives, and Chapter 9 - Local and Other Sources.

Chapter 7

Information Available from The National Archives

The National Archives

The National Archives and Records Administration (NARA) was established in 1934 and has millions of records related to the Civil War. These records are deposited in the National Archive facilities in Washington, D.C. and in the Regional Archives listed in Table 4. Most of the original Civil War records may be viewed at the National Archives in Washington, D.C. Starting in 1940, a program was begun to microfilm the records and these microfilm rolls are now available at the National Archives and its branches. In addition, copies have been purchased and are available at larger libraries, colleges, historical societies, and at the Church of the Latter-day Saints (LDS) in either Salt Lake City, Utah or at your local LDS Family History Center. Many microfilms are also available for loan or purchase through the mail from the National Archives and the American Genealogical Lending Library (AGLL). Refer to Table 6 for addresses. Recently the NARA has been working with Web sites such as Footnote, Family Search and Ancestry to digitize many of its microfilmed documents. Under a nonexclusive agreement NARA gets copies of the digitized records while the Web sites make them available for viewing and printing – sometimes for a fee.

The National Archives maintains an excellent Web site related to military records which may be used for genealogy and Civil War research: www.archives.gov/genealogy/ military

Nearly all of the records at The National Archives which are of interest to the beginning Civil War researcher have been microfilmed. The microfilm records are divided into two series designated as "M" or "T" and appears as M236, T214, etc. Generally, the "M" series includes an entire set of related records and will have an introduction that details the origin and arrangement of the records. The "T" series usually contains only a part of a record and was produced in response to a specific request. The majority of Civil War records are in the "M" series. A particular "M" or "T" file may contain from one to hundreds of rolls of microfilm. For example, M535 which is the index to compiled service records of Connecticut volunteers consists of 17 rolls of 16 mm microfilm, see Table 1. The National Archives, its branches and nearly all libraries have readers that you can use to scan and print copies of the microfilms. Many images are now available on the Internet as discussed above. One of the best resources for using these microfilms is, *Military Service Records, A Select Catalog of National Archives Microfilm Publications,* published by the National Archives. This publication is available at most libraries or through the National Archives Web site.

For the purposes of this book, Civil War records have been classified as either primary or secondary:

1. Primary records include the service records and pension records.

2. Secondary records include all other records such as prison, medical, court martial, regimental histories. etc.

Copies of the primary records such as Union and Confederate service records and Union pension records may be obtained using the "Quick Start" method as explained in Chapter 2. The problem usually encountered when ordering this information is that you do not know two of the key elements, other than his name, required to order the records from the National Archives: the man's state and military unit.

The remainder of this chapter focuses on how to find your man's state and unit so that copies of his records may be ordered from the National Archives. Also provided is a listing of some other information in the National Archives that may be useful in your research of the Civil War records.

Union Service Records

Fortunately, nearly all Union Army Volunteer compiled service records have been indexed are available on microfilm as shown in Table 1. For example, the index to the compiled service records of men from Illinois is M539 which consists of 101 rolls of microfilm. Unfortunately, there is not one all inclusive name index for all Union volunteer soldiers. Instead, the records are arranged by state and then alphabetically by surname. Therefore, if you want to find out what state he came from or what unit he was in, you must search the microfilm records for all states until you find him. This is not as bad as it sounds since usually you will have some information about his enlistment state from family records or local histories, so start with your best guess

Each state index to the compiled service records is arranged alphabetically by name and provides his branch of service, unit and company. (The actual original service records are arranged by state, unit, and name, so you can see why the staff at the National Archives needs to know the state and unit before starting the search). If you do not find the man's name in his home state or territory, it may be necessary to look in several states. It is possible that a soldier enlisted in one state but was then transferred to a unit in another state. Occasionally they assigned a man to a special unit made up of men from several states. When you have found your man's state and regiment using the indexes listed in Table 1, you will have the information needed to complete NATF Form 86 as discussed in Chapter 2. Another possible source for this information is the pension index T288 as discussed under

Pension Records. Failing all else, just use the "cut and try" approach with the CWSS discussed in Chapter 2, e.g., keep entering various states and/or units until you find your man.

Don't be surprised when you see the Confederate states listed among those providing troops to the Union cause. Thousands of men from the Southern states served in the Union army. The compiled service records for the Union volunteers from these southern states have been microfilmed and are listed in Table 2. You may wonder why the remaining Union states are not listed among the microfilmed compiled Union service records? It is because this is as far as the National Archives got with their microfilm program in the 1940s before the war and lack of funds halted the project.

If the above procedure does not give you the information on your Union Civil War ancestor it may be because he was not in the volunteer army. Nevertheless, do not give up; he may have been in the Regular Union Army, Navy or Marines. Your search will be more difficult as the service records for these branches were never compiled as had been done for the volunteer army. Check the following National Archive documents to find information for men in the following services:

Regular Army: *Registers* of *Enlistments for the Regular US Army,* M233 (81 rolls). Also, *Enlistment Papers for the Regular Army, Series* 2, 1789-1894, *Record Group* 94, *Entry 91.*

Navy: *Indexes to Rendezvous Reports (Enlistments) in the US Navy, 1861-1865,* T1098 and T1099. Also, *Abstracts of Services of Naval Officers: 1789*-1893, M330.

Marines: *Muster Rolls of U. S. Marines Corp. 1789 – 1892,* T1118. *Abstracts of Services of Naval Officers, 1789-1893, M330.* Also, *Card List Index* of *Enlisted Men in the US Marine Corps,* 1789-1941, (not available on microfilm.)

If you still have not found a reference to your ancestor, it may have been that he was in a state militia not attached to the Union forces. In this case you will only find his records in the state archives, refer to Chapter 8. Further, there are thousands of service records that were lost and never made their way into the National Archives. Therefore just because you do not find his name in the National Archives does not mean he did not fight in the Civil War. Again, check the state archives for state rosters and military histories that may at least have some mention of your ancestor's name.

There are many other references that may be searched, but a listing here is beyond the scope of this introductory book. Refer to the excellent publications listed Chapter 9 for additional avenues of research.

Union Pension Records

The original pension records are only available at the National Archives. Get copies by using NATF Form 85, see Chapter 2. If you do not know the veteran's state or unit, refer to the microfilmed *General Index to Pension Files, 1861-1934,* T288 (544 rolls). This excellent source of genealogical information is arranged alphabetically by name and each card lists unit, rank, term of service, application and certificate numbers, name of dependent(s), and state from which the claim was filed. T288 includes pension index information for the Union Volunteer and Regular Army, Navy and Marine veterans.

The pension records themselves often include genealogical gems such as marriage date and place, where they lived after the war, names and dates of children, employment, income and property. By some strange quirk pension records very seldom contain the names of the veteran's parents. You can usually extract his parent's names from the 1850 or 1860 census.

Secondary Union Records

Secondary records include a wide variety of information. Some of the more interesting secondary Civil War records available at the National Archives are listed below.

- *Compiled Records Showing Service of Military Units in Volunteer Union Organizations,* M594 (225 rolls). These records give the history of military units in voluntary Union organizations and are arranged alphabetically by state and then by unit such as cavalry, infantry or artillery. These records contain little information about individual soldiers but do provide a detailed record of the unit based on compiled papers.

- *Descriptive Lists of Colored Volunteers* 1864, (54 volumes). These records are arranged chronologically with each volume indexed by name. Lists black volunteer soldiers enlisted in the army under General Order #135.

- *Abstracts* of *Medical Records,* 1861-1865. Arranged by state, regiment and then by name.

- *Registers of Enlistment in the US Navy Rolls of Vessels, 1860-1900.*

- *Union Soldiers Buried at National Cemeteries, 1861-1865.* Arranged by state and then by name, also by cemetery and unit. Requests for information may be directed to: Director, Cemetery Service, National Cemetery System, Veterans Administration, Washington, D.C. 20422.

- *Card Index to Applications for Headstones, 1879-1903.* Also, *Applications for Headstones,* 1879-1964. These documents include the applications for headstones for Civil War veterans buried in private cemeteries. Requests for information may be directed to: The Monument Service Veterans Administration, 810 Vermont Avenue, NE Washington, D.C. 20422.

Confederate Service Records

The search of records at the National Archives for a Confederate ancestor is much easier than for a Union ancestor since all available Confederate army service records have been compiled, indexed and microfilmed. The search is further simplified because all of the names for all states have been consolidated into one name index. To find the service records for one individual, look for his name in the *Consolidated Index to Compiled Service Records of Confederate Soldiers,* M253 (535 rolls). Information is arranged alphabetically by name and includes branch of service, state, unit, company and rank. This is the information you need to request copies of the service records using NATF Form 85 as discussed in Chapter 2. If you have access to the microfilms from the National Archives, you can review and copy the compiled service records yourself. To do this, refer to Table 3 for the number of the microfilm file of compiled service records for his state, for example, Alabama is microfilm roll number M311 (508 rolls). These state records are arranged by branch of service, unit and then alphabetically by name. Since you know his unit from looking at M253, go to that unit and then search for the name. Expect to find copies of abstract cards relating to muster rolls, payrolls, medical notations, POW notations, promotions, etc.

Compiled service records for soldiers in units raised directly by the Confederate Government are available in National Archives microfilm record M258 (123 rolls). The same information for Confederate General and Staff Officers and non-regimental enlisted men is available on microfilmed record M331 (275 rolls). Names are arranged alphabetically.

The compiled service records of former Confederate soldiers who served in the Union 1st through 6th Volunteer Infantry Regiments are listed in M1017 (65 rolls). These soldiers were Confederate prisoners of war who gained their release from prison by enlisting in the Union Army. General Grant posted these "galvanized" units to the Northwestern Frontier to quell the Plains Indians so the soldiers would not have to fight against their former comrades.

If the above procedures do not give you the information on your Confederate Civil War ancestor, it may be because he was not in the army. If he was in the Confederate Navy or Marines then check the National Archives microfilm *Copies of Service, Hospital and Prison Records Relating to Confederate Naval and Marine Personnel,* M260 (7 rolls). If your man was a "blockade runner" refer to *Papers Relating to Vessels with the Confederate States of America,* M909 (32 rolls).

Confederate Pension Records

Since the Union did not give pensions to Confederate veterans, these records are not available in the National Archives. Confederate pension records are only available from states that gave pensions to their veterans and widows. Refer to Chapter 8 for instructions on how to obtain Confederate pension records from the various state archives.

Secondary Confederate Records

As stated above, secondary records include a wide variety of information. Some more interesting Confederate records available at the National Archives are listed below.

- *Compiled Records Showing Service of Military Units in Confederate Organizations,* M861 (47 rolls). These records give the history of military units in Confederate organizations and are arranged alphabetically by state and then by unit such as cavalry, infantry or artillery. This source contains little information about individual soldiers but provides a detailed record of the unit itself.

- *Selected Records of the War Department Relating to Confederate Prisoners of War, 1861-1865*, M598 *(145* rolls). Arranged alphabetically by the name of the military prison or place of confinement. Registers of prisons seldom have a complete listing of all the prisoners.

- *Copies of Registers of Confederate Soldiers, Sailors and Citizens Who Died in Federal Prisons and Military Hospitals in the North,* M918 (1 roll). Arranged by place and then by name.

- *Elements of a Good Confederate Name Search.* A handout available at the Military Reference Branch of the National Archives.

Federal Census Records

No discussion of Civil War genealogy would be complete without a reference to the information contained in the U.S. Federal Census. These population counts began in 1790 and are required every ten years by constitutional law to determine the congressional representation for each state. The census schedules through 1930 have been microfilmed and are available at the National Archives, Branch Archives, larger public libraries, LDS Family History Centers, and on the Internet. Usually, indexes to the census are also available to help in your research. Many of the microfilms are available for loan or purchase through the mail from the National Archives and the American Genealogical Lending Library (AGLL). Refer to Table 6 for addresses.

The best place to check all census records is on the Internet Web sites listed in Chapter 2

1850 Census. The 7th Federal census was recorded as of June 1, 1850 and included several enhancements of value to Civil War genealogists. For the first time the names of all free persons were recorded, not just the heads of households. Along with each name is the age, sex, color, profession of each male over 15, value of owned real-estate, value of personal property, place of birth (state or country), if married within the past year, if attended school within the past year, if over 20 and unable to read and write, and if dumb, blind, deaf, insane or a convict. The 1850 census is on National Archives M432 (1009 rolls).

1860 Census. The 8th Federal Census was recorded as of June 1, 1860 and recorded essentially the same information as the 1850 census. Available in National Archives M653 (1438 rolls).

1870 Census. The 9th Federal Census was recorded as of June 1, 1870. In addition to the information recorded in the 1860 census was: If father was foreign born, if mother was foreign born, if male citizen over 21, and if male citizen over 21 and denied the right to vote. Available in National Archives M593 (1748 rolls). The 1870 and subsequent census provide a fascinating "record trail" of what happened to your ancestor after his Civil War adventures.

1880 Census. The 10th Federal Census was taken as of June 1, 1880. Items added were: father's place of birth (state or country), mother's place of birth (state or country), relationship to head of household, if single, married, divorced or widowed, number of months unemployed in the previous year and if disabled. National Archives microfilm T9 (1454 rolls.)

1890 Census. The 1890 census included a special enumeration of Union and Confederate veterans. Unfortunately, the 1890 census is incomplete as most of the records were lost in a fire in 1921. Surviving information is available as the *Special Schedules* of *the 11th Census (1890) Enumerating Veterans and Widows* of *the Civil War Veterans.* National Archives M123 (118 rolls).

The 1910 Census is also worth checking as it shows whether a citizen was a Civil War veteran or widow of a veteran. In addition to the Federal census on the ten-year cycle, many states also conducted their own census on the off years.

There are many excellent books that will serve as your guide to genealogical research using the Federal census. A few are listed in Chapter 9 and these, along the National Archives Web site www.archives.gov/genealogy/census are a good way to start.

One final note: the commercial Web sites listed in Chapter 3 are continuously updating and adding digitized databases which can greatly enhance your ability to search the records from the National Archives. Check out these sites on a routine basis for the latest updates.

Chapter 8

Information Available from State Archives

Each state has archives where Civil War records are stored and the staff will usually respond to your request for information and copies. Addresses for all states are provided in Table 5. Most states have Web sites that provide information about their Civil War collections and how to request information Best results are obtained by sending a large self addressed stamped envelope (SASE) along with your actual request for information. Keep your questions as brief and specific as possible. To help the records' clerk find your ancestor, be sure to supply his full name, military unit, hometown and any other available information. If there is a charge for copies, they will let you know or, to save time, enclose a check for $10.

Pension Records

All of the Confederate states as well as some border states provided pensions or land grants to their Civil War veterans and these records are kept in the state archives At first, pensions were only granted to veterans who were unable to work because of disease or wounds incurred in the war, however, benefits were eventually extended to nearly all veterans and their widows. The pension records are only available in the state archives where the application was filed. Eligibility for a state pension was based on the state of residency at the time of application, not where he enlisted and served. An exception was Virginia which required residency before 1862. Eligibility and amounts varied between the Confederate states. Alabama, for example, established a Pension Commission in 1867 which provided funds for artificial arms or legs to replace limbs lost in battle. By 1891 the laws had been expanded to provide financial assistance for the veteran or his widow. Applicants had to prove desertion-free service with the Confederate forces, had to be indigent and could not own property valued at more than $2,000. Texas, however, set aside 1,280 acres of land in 1881 to be given to veterans or widows of veterans who were permanently disabled in the service of the Confederacy or the State of Texas. In 1889 the Texas law was changed to provide cash awards to veterans or their widows.

In addition to checking the state archives for pension records, check the county court house records since most pension applications required local supporting information. Many Confederate pension records have been microfilmed and are available through the Internet.

The following addresses may be used to solicit information about Confederate Pension Records:

Alabama
Alabama Department of Archives and History
624 Washington Avenue, Montgomery, AL 36130-0100
Telephone: 334-242-4363

In 1867 Alabama began granting pensions to Confederate veterans who had lost arms or legs. In 1886 the State began granting pensions to veterans' widows. In 1891 the law was amended to grant pensions to indigent veterans or their widows.

Arkansas
Arkansas History Commission
1 Capitol Mall, Little Rock, AR 72201
Telephone: 501-682-6900

In 1891 Arkansas began granting pensions to indigent Confederate veterans. In 1915 the State began granting pensions to their widows and mothers. Two published indexes are available in many libraries.

Florida
Florida State Archives
R. A. Gray Building
500 South Bronough Street, Tallahassee, FL 32399-0250
Telephone: 850-487-2073

In 1885 Florida began granting pensions to Confederate veterans. In 1889 the State began granting pensions to their widows. A published index, which provides each veteran's pension number, is available in many libraries.

Georgia
Georgia Department of Archives and History
5800 Jonesboro Road, Morrow, GA 30260
Telephone: (678) 364-3700

In 1870 Georgia began granting pensions to soldiers with artificial limbs. In 1879 the State began granting pensions to other disabled Confederate veterans or their widows who then resided in Georgia. By 1894 eligible disabilities had been expanded to include old age and poverty.

Kentucky
Kentucky Department for Libraries and Archives
Research Room
300 Coffee Tree Road, Frankfort, KY 40601
Telephone: 502-564-8704

In 1912, Kentucky began granting pensions to Confederate veterans or their widows. The records are on microfilm. A published index is available.

Louisiana
Louisiana State Archives
3851 Essen Lane, Baton Rouge, LA 70809-2137

Telephone: 504-922-1208

In 1898 Louisiana began granting pensions to indigent Confederate veterans or their widows.

Mississippi
Mississippi Department of Archives and History
P.O. Box 571, Jackson, MS 39205
Telephone: 601-359-6876

In 1888 Mississippi began granting pensions to indigent Confederate veterans or their widows. A published index is available.

Missouri
Missouri State Archives
600 W. Main, P.O. Box 1747
Jefferson City, MO 65102
Telephone: 573-751-3280

In 1911 Missouri began granting pensions to indigent Confederate veterans only; none were granted to widows. Missouri also had a home for disabled Confederate veterans. The pension and veterans' home applications are interfiled and arranged alphabetically.

North Carolina
North Carolina State Archive
109 East Jones Street, Raleigh, NC 27601-2807
Telephone: 919-733-7305

In 1867 North Carolina began granting pensions to Confederate veterans who were blinded or lost an arm or leg during their service. In 1885 the State began granting pensions to all other disabled indigent Confederate veterans and widows.

Oklahoma
Oklahoma Department of Libraries
Archives and Records Management Divisions
200 Northeast 18th Street, Oklahoma City, OK 73105

Telephone: 1-800-522-8116, ext. 209

In 1915 Oklahoma began granting pensions to Confederate veterans or their widows. A published index is available:

South Carolina
South Carolina Department of Archives and History
301 Parkland Road, Columbia, SC 29223
Telephone: 803-896-6100

A state law enacted in 1887 permitted financially needy Confederate veterans and widows to apply for a pension, however, few applications survive from the 1888-1918 era. Beginning in 1889, the SC Comptroller began publishing lists of such veterans receiving pensions in his *Annual Report*. From 1919 to 1925, South Carolina granted pensions to Confederate veterans and widows regardless of financial need. These files are arranged alphabetically. Also available are Confederate Home applications and inmate records for veterans (1909-1957), and applications of wives, widows, sisters, and daughters (1925-1955).

Tennessee
Tennessee State Library and Archives
Public Service Division
403 Seventh Avenue North, Nashville, TN 37243-0312
Telephone: 615-741-2764

In 1891 Tennessee began granting pensions to indigent Confederate veterans. In 1905 the State began granting pensions to their widows. The records are on microfilm. A published index is available:

Texas
Texas State Library and Archives Commission
Genealogy and Archives & Manuscripts
P.O. Box 12927, Austin, TX 7871
Telephone: 512-463-5480

In 1881 Texas set aside 1,280 acres for disabled Confederate veterans. In 1889 the State began granting pensions to indigent Confederate veterans and their widows. Muster rolls of State militia in Confederate service are also available. A published index is available:

Virginia
Library of Virginia Archives Division
800 East Broad Street, Richmond, VA 23219
Telephone: 804-692-3888

Virginia began granting pensions to Confederate veterans or their widows in 1888. The records are on microfilm.

Note: Source for addresses and status is: The National Archives Web site

Service records
If you know or suspect that your ancestor was in the Civil War but have not been able to find any information on him at the National Archives, it may be that he was in a state militia. Most states had militia, now called the National Guard, which fought mostly within the state boundaries and were never attached to the Union or Confederate forces. If your man was in a state militia, the state archives will be a source for his service records. Check the state archives Web sites listed in Table 5 for availability of records.

Other Information

Many states published or backed the publication of the history of their military actions in the Civil War, e.g., *Texas in the War,* 1861-1865, or *Michigan in the Civil War.* Copies of these publications can usually be found in the collections of the state archives. Also check, *Military Bibliography* of *the Civil War,* by Charles Dornbush for a listing of all military unit histories.

Military rosters were published by most states listing the name and military unit of men and women who served in the Civil War, e.g., *Roster* of *Confederate Soldiers* of *Georgia,*

Roster of *NC Troops in the War Between the States,* and *Records of Officers and Men* of *New Jersey in the Civil War.* Again, these rosters will be found in the collections of the state archives and may have been microfilmed.

Toward the end of the 1800's, it was common for publishing companies to print city and county histories that contained biographies of distinguished persons. Or, at least those willing to pay to have their biography included. If your ancestor was an officer or a famous person, chances are that he will be listed in these publications which are actually a wonderful source of information about the man, his family and Civil War actions. Many of these city/county vanity publications have been microfilmed are available in public libraries.

Another source of information is the mortality census conducted by most states in the five years between Federal censuses. Most of the state census reports are available on the Internet.

Chapter 9

Information from Other Sources

There are literally hundreds of publications about the Civil War, and even nearly 150 years later, the list continues to grow. Some of the more useful publications are listed below. Your local librarian can help you locate and obtain copies. Often, publications not available in your local library can be obtained through the interlibrary loan program. The following is a discussion of publications of interest to anyone doing Civil War genealogy and research. Always check the Internet sites listed in Chapter 3 to see if these or new publications have become available on the Internet.

Probably the largest collection of Civil War documents is contained in the *Official Records of the Union and Confederate Armies in the War* of *the Rebellion,* Government Printing Office, 140,000 pages contained in 128 volumes. This publication is sometimes called the Official Record (OR) and includes all Union and Confederate documents gathered by the War Department at the end of the war. This publication is available on microfilm M262, arranged by state, Union or Confederate and then by military unit. There is a similar set of 31 volumes of naval records, *Official Record* of *Union and Confederate Navies in the War* of *the Rebellion, the ORN.* The ORN is arranged by ship. Because the OR and ORN are such important records, you will find them in most libraries. If not, they are available from the interlibrary loan program. The OR is now available on the Internet and as a CD for computers.

The *Official Atlas of the Civil War* includes maps of battlefields, towns and marching routes drawn and used during the Civil War.

The Grand Army of the Republic (GAR) was organized in 1866 and had 409,000 Union members at its height in 1890. The GAR was organized into state departments that were subdivided into about 6,000 camps. The GAR was dissolved in the 1950's and all of their records and publications were eventually turned over to the Library of Congress where they are available for review.

The *Sons and Daughters of Union Veterans* remains active; their address is 503 S. Walnut Street, Springfield, IL 62703.

The United Confederate Veterans (UCV) was the largest Southern veterans' organization with about 65,000 members. Their records are contained in a 40-volume collection, *The Confederate Veteran,* available at larger research organizations.

The Sons of Confederate Veterans (SCV) still has many active local chapters. Their address is P.O. Box 59, Columbia, TN 38401

Another source of Confederate information is the library of the United Daughters of the Confederacy in Richmond, Virginia. This organization has a long, rich history and is still active. Address is 328 N. Boulevard, Richmond, VA 23220.

Southern Historical Society Papers, 52 volumes with a two volume index that includes names. Published by the Southern Historical Society in Richmond, Virginia.

Military Service Records: A Select Catalog of *National Archives Microfilm Publications,* 1985. This publication printed by the National Archives Trust Fund is a must for serious Civil War research. Available from the National Archives and most libraries.

An excellent guide to Civil War publications is *Military Bibliography of the Civil War,* three volumes, by Charles Dornbusch. This reference book may be found in large libraries and lists nearly all of the unit history publications. If you are doing detailed research on a particular unit, check this publication first.

The US Army Military History Institute at Carlisle, Pennsylvania has an excellent library of Civil War unit histories. If you know your ancestor's unit, send a large SASE to the following address and they will send you information on available documents: Reference Branch, The US Army Military History Institute, Carlisle Barracks, PA 17013. Or, if you are in the Gettysburg, Pennsylvania area and enjoy doing your own research, a side trip to the Institute is well worth the time.

In the 1890's, many cities and counties published local histories that included biographical information about their Civil War veterans, many of whom had by then achieved the status of "prominent citizens." These biographies can be a valuable source of genealogical information but should be regarded with some suspicion since the authors tended to fluff the product to sell the books. Many of these publications have been microfilmed by the Daughters of the American Revolution and are available at larger libraries and genealogical collections.

Confederate Research Center at Hill College, PO Box 619, Hillsboro, Texas 76645. This facility has an excellent collection and a helpful staff.

The Civil War historical sites supervised by the National Park Service can provide much information about specific battlefields. Some sites now have computerized files listing the servicemen who fought at that particular battlefield.

Most local newspapers published detailed accounts of the reunions of the Civil War veterans, including the names of the attendees. Also, if you know the death date of your ancestor, the newspaper obituaries can provide a wealth of information.

The local court house may have death certificates that usually list parents' names and cause of death. In addition they have marriage, deed, tax and enlistment records. Check Everton's *Handy Book for Genealogists* for court house address where you can write for this information.

A visit to the cemetery where your ancestor is buried can be a source of information as well as a moving experience. Civil War grave markers were usually an upright slab engraved with the veteran's name and unit. Union graves are often marked with a special marker, usually bronze with a five pointed star, "GAR1861-1865". The points of the star are marked with the insignia of the infantry, cavalry, artillery and signal for the army, and the insignia of the navy. Several local genealogical societies have compiled name indexes for cemeteries which can save you hours when looking for a particular grave. In addition, they have published GPS coordinates to help you find the cemetery.

Many Civil War genealogists think that finding their African roots is impossible. However, if he was in the Union Army his records should be in the National Archives as mentioned in Chapter 7. Start your search by looking in the *Index to Colored Troops*, M589 (see table 1). Also, refer to *Black Roots – a Beginners Guide to Tracing the African-American Family Tree* by Tony Burroughs. Another source is, *Black Family Research: Records of Post Civil War Federal Agencies*. Available at the National Archives. Ancestry.com has images of the 1850 and 1860 Slave Schedules.

Additional sources of Civil War information are: local historical societies and libraries, city and county histories, Civil War periodicals and local genealogical societies.

Many communities have an active "Civil War Round Table" where the local Civil War buffs gather to hear speakers and to discuss the battles and strategies. If you are just getting started in Civil War genealogy, the Round Table can be a valuable source of information. Web site **www.civilwar.com** includes a list of Civil War Round Tables and reenactments searchable by state and city.

Chapter 10

The Civil War Soldiers and Sailors System (A Computerized Database)

The Civil War Soldiers and Sailors System (CWSS) is a computerized database with military service records of 6.3 million names of both Union and Confederate soldiers and sailors who served in the Civil War. There were actually about 3.5 million men and women in the war but the discrepancy comes about because a separate record was generated each time a soldier served in a different unit, served under two names, etc. A successful search of the CWSS yields the soldier's rank, military unit, company and a roster listing all of the men in his unit. It also provides a history of his unit with links to its major battles. This first phase of the CWSS, the Name Index for Union and Confederate soldiers, was essentially completed in 2004 and marked with a special ceremony at Ford's Theater in Washington, DC.

The CWSS is a continuing work in progress. The soldiers Name Index described above is essentially complete although additional names will be added as they surface. Efforts are underway to include Union and Confederate Naval personnel. This will be a more difficult process as the naval records are not as well organized and have not been microfilmed. The Prisoners Section will be expanded to include the history of all Union and Confederate prisons and the names of the prisoners. Links to the National Park Service Civil War sites will also be added. As funds permit, the CWSS will include information on the thousands of Civil War monuments as well as links to the 14 National Cemeteries with lists of burials.

Using the System

The CWSS database can be accessed at the National Park Service Web site **www.itd.nps.gov/cwss**. The system is self explanatory and very easy to use: Select "Soldiers" and enter as much information as you have including last name, first name, Union or Confederate, state of origin, military unit, and function such as infantry, cavalry, sharpshooter or engineer. You don't have to enter all of this information to get some results, just start with whatever information you have. Assuming that you know his name and whether Confederate or Union, you may not know his state or unit. In this case you may have to spend some time checking family records, old letters, diaries, local histories, and visits to your local library or make an educated guess at his home state and unit, enter it in the CWSS online form and hope for the best. If you have no clues as to service branch, keep in mind that the vast majority of men were in the volunteer army infantry. Unfortunately, only a portion of the Union and Confederate sailors are now included in the CWSS. Likewise, the CWSS does not include records for those in the Regular Army or state militia.

A Visit to a Civil War National Park

When fully implemented it will be possible for a visitor at one of the Civil War National Parks to enter the name of their Civil War ancestor into a computer and receive a listing of his regiment, rank and state from which he served. In addition, CWSS will be able to help answer one of the most frequently asked questions at the Civil War National Park Visitor Centers, (other than "Where is the rest room?"), "Did my ancestor fight at this battlefield?" Retrieval of this information will be possible since the database will eventually include a summary history of over 4,000 regiments that fought in 10,000 engagements and 500 battles during the Civil War. Thus by knowing what regiment your man was in and calling up the regimental history on the computer, you will be able to make some fairly safe assumptions about his participation at a particular battle site. A word of caution however, the fact that he was in a certain regiment, i.e. 3rd Indiana Infantry, should not be used as proof that he fought at a specific battle such as the Battle of Gettysburg. He may have been on sick call, temporary duty at another location, on furlough, etc. Plans also call for the database to include Civil War burial records as well. So if your ancestor was buried at that site, you can walk outside and visit his grave. If he was buried at another National Cemetery or if his heirs applied for a headstone in another cemetery, you can also find the location.

Source of the CWSS Records

The source for the information in the CWSS database is the General Index Cards which were created by the Department of the Army in the 1880s to help determine eligibility for pensions. These cards were based on muster rolls which were taken by each military unit about every two weeks. When the records were compiled in the 1880s, an index card was created for each time a soldiers' name appeared on a muster roll. These in turn were summarized on the General Index Card and listed the soldier's name, rank at the time of enlistment from the first card and date and rank at time of separation from the last card. Because some soldiers served in more than one unit or served under two different names, this process generated about 6.3 million records from the approximately 3.5 million soldiers actually in the war.

The CWSS database is a joint project of The National Parks Service, The National Archives, The Genealogical Society of Utah (GSU) and The Federation of Genealogical Societies (FGS). These organizations spread the database entry work among hundreds of volunteers who spent countless hours entering and verifying the results. Truly this is one of the biggest archival and genealogical success stories of our times.

Chapter 11

Using DNA to Find Your Civil War Ancestors

In recent years, Deoxyribonucleic Acid (DNA) has become an important tool in tracing family genealogies and many researchers are now using DNA to complement traditional genealogical resources. Here is a story to illustrate how a fictional Bill Smith used DNA to find his Civil War heritage.

Bill, a young man in his twenties, was attending a business conference. One day during the lunch break he wandered into the town square where he noticed a statue flanked by two Civil War cannons. The statue was of a Civil War general seated on a horse. The green crusted copper plate on the base read, "General William Smith 1834 - 1863. Killed at the Battle of Gettysburg".

After struggling a few minutes trying to dredge up his high school history class lessons about the Battle of Gettysburg, Bill suddenly realized that his name was the same as General William Smith. Could they be related? But Bill, being an orphan raised at a State Orphanage, knew nothing of his family let alone a possible relation to General Smith. Back at the conference, Bill mentioned the statue to an associate, the coincidence of names and his interest in finding his family roots. The wise classmate, being a seasoned genealogist, said, "Maybe you can use a DNA test to find out if you are related."

Let us digress for a few minutes from Bill's problem to review the mechanics of DNA. As you remember from your high school biology class, each cell contains a nucleus with a packet of genetic material which has instructions on how the cell and indeed, the whole body, operate. DNA is found within the nucleus of each cell and is tightly wrapped in configurations known as chromosomes. If you were to unravel a strand of DNA it would be about six feet long. Humans have 46 chromosomes grouped into 23 pairs and each pair is composed of one chromosome from each of our parents. Each of the chromosome pairs has a different set of instructions which tells the cell what to do. Further, each chromosome is divided into sections called genes that have sequences of information that determines inherited characteristics. The first 22 of the 23 chromosome pairs in males and females are much the same. The 23rd chromosome pair, however, differs between the sexes and determines our gender. This pair consists of either an XX (female) or an XY (male) combination. The Y-chromosome in the 23rd pair does not mingle with the X-chromosome and thus stays the same through the generations unless a mutation occurs. Therefore the son has the same Y-chromosome as his father, grandfather, etc. and can be used to verify relationships. Again this assumes that few if any mutations occur.

There are several DNA tests that can be done for genealogical purposes but the most commonly used is the Y-chromosome test because it combines DNA analysis with family surnames. Passed directly from father to son in the 23 chromosome pair without combining with the female X-chromosome, the Y-chromosome remains virtually unchanged from generation to generation. Further, because there are very few mutations on the Y-chromosome, examining the chromosome of a living male surname family representative will reveal information about his preceding male ancestors both living and deceased. In our western culture surnames such as Smith are passed through the father (parental line) so Y-chromosome testing achieves its best success if combined with genealogy to prove or disprove a relationship between two males, living or deceased, with the same or similar surname. Females can obtain the same results by having a close male family member such as father, brother or paternal uncle submit a test for them. Thus, where there is a proven family line we have an opportunity to facilitate the discovery of genetic relatives.

The most common ways of using the resulting Y-chromosome test results for genealogical research are: 1) family surname projects, 2) DNA database matching, and 3) Y-chromosome Haplogroups. These are discussed below:

1. There are several DNA surname projects which can be accessed on the Internet, each hosted by a coordinator who helps bring together genetic cousins and to explore family genealogies.

2. Y-chromosome test results may also be used to search for genetic cousins by querying large Y-chromosome databases accessible on the Internet. These searches are able to compare up to 46 separate markers on the Y-chromosome.

3. Y-chromosome Haplogroups can be thought of as branches of the genetic tree with roots in Africa approximately 140,000 years ago. Over the years small mutations occurred on the Y-chromosome and these can be thought of as branches on the genetic tree. These branches became more pronounced as people migrated into different continents and regions. Dozens of Haplogroups have been identified as people migrated to different parts of the world and as small mutations of the Y-chromosome took place. For example, the results of my Y-chromosome test indicated that my Haplogroup is R1b which is a subgroup of Haplogroup R1. The people of R1 first arrived in Europe from West Africa during the Upper Paleolithic period 35,000 to 40,000 years ago. The mutation which defines R1b likely developed within the Iberian Peninsula and moved north and west with the end of the ice age. Haplogroup R1 is found in about 50% of Europeans whereas R1b is by far the

most common Haplogroup in Western Europe (Spain, Portugal, France, England and Ireland).

Now, with that background on how DNA is used in genealogy, let's return to Bill Smith and the search for his roots and possible relationship to General William Smith.

Of course there was no way that Bill could obtain a DNA sample from General Smith without being thrown in jail for an unspeakable crime committed in the graveyard on a very dark night. But, if he could find a living male relative descendant of the town hero who was willing to submit a DNA sample, there was a very good chance that he could prove or disprove the relationship. And if successful, find the key to his family roots. At the Genealogy Section of the local library, Bill found a book with the biography of General Smith including a list of his descendants. Explaining his problem to the librarian, Bill was able to find the name and telephone number of a living male descendant of General Smith.

To make a long story short, both Bill and what turned out to be his long lost cousin submitted a DNA sample consisting of a simple cheek swab costing less than $75. The results indicated that there was a statistical confident level of 96 percent that their most recent common ancestor (MRCA) was four generations back, to the time of their great great grandfather, General W. Smith.

Elated by his discovery, Bill skipped out of his meetings and, having read Chapter 2 of this book, spent the afternoon using the Internet to find and view his GG grandfather's service and pension records and to learn the history of General Smith's regiment and how he died at the Battle of Gettysburg.

If the subject of our story had been Jane rather than Bill Smith, the process would be much the same except, being female with no Y chromosome DNA, Jane could use one of two approaches to find her relationship to General Smith.

First, she could ask her father, brother or male paternal cousin, to submit a DNA sample. An analysis of his DNA as described for Bill would prove or disprove the relationship.

Second, if she had no male relatives able to take the Y-DNA test or if General Smith had only daughters (daughtered out), she could request another type of DNA test referred to as a mitochondrial DNA or mtDNA test. This test, although more complicated, expensive, and less definitive, could be used as a last resort to verify a relationship to General Smith. How is this possible given the above explanation of the 23rd chromosome? Mother Nature very cleverly provides an answer. It turns out that within in the cell wall but outside of the nucleus, there are tiny mitochondrial packets which do not mingle with the X or Y chromosomes and are passed unchanged directly from the mother to her male and female offspring. Much like the Y-chromosome, the mtDNA mutates very little through the generations and can be used following the same general procedure as described for the Y-chromosome analysis. In Jane's case, she would need to submit an mtDNA sample and to ask that a proven descendant of General Smith do the same.

This is, obviously, a very high level introduction to the new and exciting world of genealogy using DNA. There are many good books which deal with the subject such as *Trace Your Roots with DNA* by Megan Smolenyak and Ann Turner, and *Genealogy for Dummies*

A word of caution. DNA testing, although generally accepted by modern genealogists and the courts, is not an exact science but is based on statistics and probabilities. And, you know what that can mean. Also, be aware that in a few cases, people taking these DNA test have been surprised or dismayed by the results. Maybe "he" is not really your father. And, who could ever guess what skeletons are hidden in the family closet?

TABLE 1
Microfilmed Indexes to Compiled Service Records
for Union Army Volunteers

Note: Each state index is arranged alphabetically by name and provides branch of service, unit and company.

State	Index
Alabama	M263
Arizona Terr.	M532
Arkansas	M383
California	M533
Colorado Terr.	M534
Connecticut	M535
Dakota Terr.	M536
Delaware	M537
D.C.	M538
Florida	M264
Georgia	M385
Idaho	*
Illinois	M539
Indiana	M540
Iowa	M541
Kansas	M542
Kentucky	M386
Louisiana	M387
Maine	M543
Maryland	M388
Massachusetts	M544
Michigan	M545
Minnesota	M546
Mississippi	M389
Missouri	M390

Montana	*
Nebraska Terr.	M547
Nevada	M548
New Hampshire	M549
New Jersey	M550
New Mexico Terr.	M242
New York	M551
North Carolina	M391
North Dakota	M536
Ohio	M552
Oklahoma	*
Oregon	M553
Pennsylvania	M554
Rhode Island	M555
South Carolina	none
South Dakota	M536
Tennessee	M392
Texas	M393
Utah Terr.	M556
Vermont	M557
Virginia	M394
Washington Terr.	M558
West Virginia	M507
Wisconsin	M559
Wyoming	*
US Colored Troops	M589
US Reserve Corps	M636
US Volunteers	M1017

• See Washington Territory

TABLE 2
Microfilmed Compiled Service Records for Union Soldiers from Southern States (Note)

Each state compiled service record is arranged by branch of service, unit and then alphabetically by name.

State	Compiled Service Records
Alabama	M276
Arkansas	M399
Florida	M400
Georgia	M403
Kentucky	M397
Louisiana	M396
Maryland	M384
Mississippi	M404
Missouri	M405
New Mexico Ter.	M427
North Carolina	M401
Tennessee	M395
Texas	M402
Utah Terr.	M692
Virginia	M398
W. Virginia	M508
US Volunteers	M1017

Note: The compiled service records of Union Soldiers from the Northern States were never microfilmed.

TABLE 3
Microfilmed Indexes and Compiled Service Records
for
The Confederate Army

Each state <u>index</u> is arranged alphabetically by soldier's name and provides the branch of service and unit. Each <u>compiled service record</u> is arranged by branch of service, unit, and then alphabetically by name.

State	Index	Compiled Service Record
All States	M253*	nla
Alabama	M374	M311
Arizona Terr.	M375	M318
Arkansas	M376	M317
Florida	M225	M251
Georgia	M226	M266
Kentucky	M377	M319
Louisiana	M378	M320
Maryland	M379	M321
Mississippi	M232	M269
Missouri	M380	M322
North Carolina	M230	M270
South Carolina	M381	M267
Tennessee	M231	M268
Texas	M227	M323
Virginia	M382	M324
Units raised by the Confederate Government	M818	M258
General and Staff Officers	M818	M331

* M253 (535 rolls) has all soldiers for all states included in one index arranged alphabetically by name.

TABLE 4
Addresses for the National Archives and Regional Branches

For current information on NARA facilities, go to **www.archives. gov/facilities**.

National Archives

National Archives and Records Administration
Mailing Address: 800 Pennsylvania Avenue, NW, Washington, DC 20408-0001
inquire@nara.gov
www.archives.gov

National Archives and Records Administration
Mailing Address: 8601 Adelphi Road, College Park, MD 20740-6001
inquire@nara.gov
www.archives.gov

NARA Regional Archives

ANCHORAGE, ALASKA NARA-Pacific Alaska Region
Mailing Address: 654 West Third Avenue, Anchorage, AK 99501-2145
alaska.archives@nara.gov
www.archives.gov/pacific-alaska/anchorage
Serves Alaska

ATLANTA, GEORGIA NARA-Southeast Region
Mailing Address: 5780 Jonesboro Road, Morrow, GA 30260-3806
atlanta.archives@nara.gov
www.archives.gov/southeast
Serves Alabama, Florida, Georgia, Kentucky, Mississippi, North Carolina, South Carolina, and Tennessee.

BOSTON, MASSACHUSETTS NARA-Northeast Region (Boston)
Mailing Address: 380 Trapelo Road, Waltham, MA 02452-6399
waltham.archives@nara.gov

www.archives.gov/northeast/waltham/
Serves Connecticut, Maine, Massachusetts, New Hampshire, Rhode Island, and Vermont.

CHICAGO, ILLINOIS   NARA-Great Lakes Region (Chicago)
Mailing Address: 7358 South Pulaski Road, Chicago, IL 60629-5898
chicago.archives@nara.gov
www.archives.gov/great-lakes/chicago
Serves Illinois, Indiana, Michigan, Minnesota, Ohio, and Wisconsin

DENVER, COLORADO   NARA-Rocky Mountain Region
Mailing Address: Denver Federal Center, Building 48
West Sixth Avenue and Kipling Street
P.O. Box 25307, Denver, CO 80225
denver.archives@nara.gov
www.archives.gov/rocky-mountain
Serves Colorado, Montana, New Mexico, North Dakota, South Dakota, Utah, Wyoming.

FORT WORTH, TEXAS   NARA-Southwest Region
Mailing Address: 501 West Felix Street,
P.O. Box 6216, Fort Worth, TX 76115-0216
ftworth.archives@nara.gov
www.archives.gov/southwest
Serves Arkansas, Louisiana, Oklahoma, and Texas.

KANSAS CITY, MISSOURI NARA-Central Plains Region (Kansas City)
Mailing Address: 400 West Pershing Road Kansas City, MO 64108
kansascity.archives@nara.gov
*www.archives.gov/central-plains/*kansas-city
Serves Iowa, Kansas, Missouri, and Nebraska.

LAGUNA NIGUEL, CALIFORNIA NARA-Pacific Region (Laguna Niguel)
Mailing Address: 24000 Avila Road, Laguna Niguel, CA 92677-3497
laguna.archives@nara.gov

www.archives.gov/pacific/iaguna
Serves Arizona, Southern California, and Clark County, Nevada.

NEW YORK, NEW YORK   NARA-Northeast Region
Mailing Address: 201 Varick Street, 12th Floor, New York, NY 10014-4811
newyork.archives@nara.gov
www.archives.gov/northeast/nyc
Serves New Jersey, New York, Puerto Rico, and the U.S. Virgin Islands.

PHILADELPHIA, PENNSYLVANIA NARA-Mid Atlantic Region
Mailing Address: 900 Market Street, Philadelphia, PA 19107-4292
philadelphia.archives@nara.gov
 www.archives.gov/midatlantic
Serves Pennsylvania, Delaware, West Virginia, Maryland and Virginia.

PITTSFIELD, MASSACHUSETTS   NARA-Northeast Region
Mailing Address: 10 Conte Drive, Pittsfield, MA 01201-8230
Pittsfield.archives@nara.gov
www.archives.gov/northeast/pittsfield

SAN FRANCISCO, CALIFORNIA   NARA-Pacific Region
Mailing Address: 1000 Commodore Drive, San Bruno, CA 94066-2350
sanbruno.archives@nara.gov
www.archives.gov/pacific/san-francisco
Serves northern and central California, Nevada (except Clark County), Hawaii, American Samoa, and the Trust Territory of the Pacific Islands.

SEATTLE, WASHINGTON NARA-Pacific Alaska Region
Mailing Address: 6125 Sand Point Way, NE, Seattle, WA 98115-7999
seattle archives@nara.gov
www.archives.gov/pacific-alaska/seattle
Serves Idaho, Oregon, and Washington

TABLE 5
Addresses for State Archives

Alabama Department of Archives & History
624 Washington Avenue, Montgomery, AL 36130
Mailing Address: P.O. Box 300100, Montgomery, AL 36130
Phone: Reference: (334) 242-4435

Alaska State Archives
Mailing Address: P.O. Box 110525, 141 Willoughby Avenue,
Juneau, AK 99801
archives@eed.state.ak.us

Arizona State Library, Archives and Public Records
Arizona History and Archives Division
Mailing Address: State Capitol, Suite 342, 1700 West
Washington, Phoenix, AZ 85007
http://www.lib.az.us/archives/email.asp

Arkansas History Commission
Mailing Address: One Capitol Mall, Little Rock, AR 77201
Phone: (501) 682-6900

California State Archives
Mailing Address: 1020 "O" Street, Sacramento, CA 95814
ArchivesWeb@ss.ca.gov

Colorado State Archives
Mailing Address: 1313 Sherman Street, Room 1B-20, Denver,
CO 80203 archives@state.co.us

Connecticut State Archives
Mailing Address: Connecticut State Library, 231 Capitol Avenue, Hartford, CT 06106
Phone: History and Genealogy Unit: (860) 757-6580

Delaware Public Archives
mailing address: 121 Duke of York Street, Dover, DE 19901
archives@state.de.us

Florida Bureau of Archives & Records Management, Division of Library & Information Services
Mailing address: 500 South Bronough Street, Tallahassee, FL 32399
barm@dos.state.fl.us

Georgia State Archives
Mailing Address: 5800 Jonesboro Road, Morrow, GA 30260
http://www.georgiaarchives.org/menu/contact_

Hawaii Historic Records Branch
Mailing Address: Kekauluohi Building, Iolani Palace Grounds, Honolulu, HI 96813
archives@hawaii.gov

Idaho State Historical Society Library & Archives
Mailing Address: 2205 Old Penitentiary Road, Boise, ID 83712
sbarrett@ishs.state.id.us

Illinois State Archives
Mailing Address: Norton Building, Capitol Complex, Springfield, IL 62756
www.ilsos.gov/GenealogyMWeb/refform.html

Indiana State Archives
Mailing Address: 6440 East 30th Street, Indianapolis, Indiana 46219 arc@icpr.in.gov

Iowa State Library of Iowa
Mailing Address: Ola Babcock Miller Building, 1112 E. Grand
Ave., Des Moines, IA 50319-0233
www.statelibraryofiowa.org/services/askalibrarian

Kansas State Historical Society
Mailing Address: 6425 Southwest Sixth Avenue, Topeka, KS
66615
information@kshs.org

Kentucky Department for Libraries & Archives
Mailing Address: P.O. Box 537, Frankfort, KY 40602
Phone: (502) 564-8300

Louisiana State Archives
Mailing Address: 3851 Essen Lane, Baton Rouge, LA 70809
archives@sos.louisiana.gov

Maine State Archives
Mailing Address: 84 State House Station, Augusta, ME 04333-0084
anthony.douin@maine.gov

Maryland State Archives
Mailing Address: 350 Rowe Boulevard, Annapolis, MD 21401
 archives@mdsa.net

Massachusetts Archives
Mailing Address: Secretary of Commonwealth, Massachusetts
Archives, 220 Morrissey Boulevard, Boston, MA 02125
archives@sec.state.ma.us

Michigan Department of History, Arts and Libraries
Mailing Address: Archives of Michigan, 702 Kalamazoo Street,
P.O. Box 30740
archives@michigan.gov

Minnesota State Archives
Mailing Address: Minnesota Historical Society, 345 Kellogg Boulevard West, St. Paul, MN 55102
archives@mnhs.org

Mississippi Department of Archives & History
Mailing Address: P.O. Box 571, Jackson, MS 39205-0571
refdesk@mdah.state.ms.us.

Missouri State Archives
Mailing Address: 600 W. Main, P.O. Box 1747, Jefferson City, MO 65102
archref@sos.mo.gov

Montana Historical Society
Mailing Address: P.O. Box 201201, 225 North Roberts Street, Helena, MT 59620
mhslibrary@mt.gov

Nebraska Library/Archives Division
Mailing Address: Nebraska State Historical Society, P.O. Box 82554, 1500 R Street, Lincoln, NE 68501
lanshs@nebraskahistory.org

Nevada State Library & Archives
Mailing Address: 100 North Stewart Street, Carson City, NV 89701
sesearcy@clan.lib.nv.us

New Hampshire Archives & Records Management
Mailing Address: 71 South Fruit Street, Concord, NH 03301
Phone: (603) 271-2236

New Mexico State Records Center & Archives
Mailing Address: 1205 Camino Carlos Rey, Santa Fe, NM 87505 archives@state.nm.us

New Jersey Public Records and Archives
Mailing Address: State Archives: 225 West State Street-Level 2, P.O. Box 307, Trenton, NJ 08625
records.management@sos.state.nj.us

New York State Archives
Mailing Address: New York State Education Department, Cultural Education Center, Albany, NY 12230
archref@mail.nysed.gov

North Carolina State Archives
Mailing Address: 4614 Mail Service Center, Raleigh, NC 27699-4614
archives@ncmail.net

North Dakota State Archives & Historical Research Library
Mailing Address: 612 East Boulevard Avenue, Bismarck, ND 58505-0830
archives@state.nd.us

Ohio Historical Society, Archives/Library
Mailing Address: Research Services Department, 1982 Velma Avenue, Columbus, OH 43211
reference@ohiohistory.org

Oklahoma State Archives
Mailing Address: 200 Northeast Eighteenth Street, Oklahoma City, OK 73105-3298
www.odl.state.ok.us/oar/contacts/index.html

Oregon State Archives
Mailing Address: 800 Summer Street NE, Salem, OR 97310
reference.archives@state.or.us

Pennsylvania State Archives
Mailing Address: 350 North Street, Harrisburg, PA 17120-0090
www.phmc.state.pa.us/bah.dam/mailreflet.html

Rhode Island State Archives
Mailing Address: 337 Westminster Street, Providence, RI 02903
reference@sec.state.ri.us

South Carolina State Archives & History Center
Mailing Address: 8301 Parklane Road, Columbia, SC 29223
www.state.sc.us/scdah/refquery.htm

South Dakota State Archives
Mailing Address: 900 Governors Drive, Pierre, SD 57501-2217
archref@state.sd.us

Tennessee State Library & Archives
Mailing Address: 403 Seventh Avenue North, Nashville, TN 37243-0312
reference.tsla@state.tn.us

Texas State Library & Archives Commission
Mailing Address: P.O. Box 12927, Austin, TX 78711
reference.desk@tsl.state.tx.us

Utah State Archives
Mailing Address: Utah State Archives, 346 S Rio Grande, Salt Lake City, UT 84101-1106
www.historyresearch.utah.gov/question.htm

Vermont State Archives
Mailing Address: Office of the Secretary of State, 26 Terrace Street, Montpelier, VT 05609-1101
archives@sec.state.vt.us

Virginia Archives Research Services
Mailing Address: Library of Virginia, 800 East Broad Street,
Richmond, VA 23219
www.lva.lib.va.us/whatwedo/archemailform.asp

Washington State Archives
Mailing Address: P.O. Box 40238, Olympia, WA 98504
archives@secstate.wa.gov

West Virginia State Archives
Mailing Address: Archives & History Library 1900 Kanawha
Boulevard East, Charleston, WV 25305
Phone: (304) 558-0230

Wisconsin State Historical Society
Mailing Address: Archives Reference, 816 State Street,
Madison, WI 53706 www.wisconsinhistory.org/libraryarchives

Wyoming State Archives
Mailing Address: Barrett Building, 2301 Central Avenue,
Cheyenne, WY 82002
wyarchive@state.wy.us

Source: National Archiveshttp://www.archives.gov/research/
alic/reference/state-archives.html

Table 6
Addresses for Additional Information

Ancestry Publishing
P.O. Box 476
Salt Lake City, UT 84110

American Genealogical Lending Library (AGLL)
P.O. Box 329
Bountiful, UT 84011

Church of Jesus Christ of Latter-day Saints LDS Family History Center
35 North West Temple Street
Salt Lake City, UT 84150
Phone 801 240-2584
Also, check your phone directory for
one of the 670 local Family History Centers.

Confederate Research Center Hillsboro College
PO Box 619,
Hill, Texas 76645

Daughters of the Union Civil War
Suite 525, 2025 Pennsylvania Avenue NW
Washington, D.C. 20006

Everton Publishers, Inc.
P.O. Box 368
Logan, UT 84323

Federation of Genealogical Societies
P.O. Box 3385
Salt Lake City. UT 84110-3385

Genealogical Publishing Co.
1001 N. Calvert St.
Baltimore, MD 21202

Museum of the Confederacy
1201 E. Clay Street
Richmond, VA 23219

National Archives
8th and Pennsylvania Ave. NW
Washington, D.C. 20408

National Cemetery System Veterans Administration
Washington, D.C. 20420

National Genealogical Society
4527 17th St. North
Arlington, VA 22207

United Daughters of the Confederacy
328 N. Boulevard
Richmond. VA 23220

United States Army Military History Institute Civil War Reference Branch
Carlisle Barracks, PA 17013.

Bibliography

Allen, Desmond W. *Where to Write for Confederate Pension Records.* Bryant, Arkansas: Research Associates, 1991.

Beers, Henry P. *Guide to the Archives* of *the Government the Confederate States* of *America.* National Archives Publication No. 68-15. Washington, D.C.: Government Printing Office, 1968.

Beers, Henry P. and Munden, Kenneth W. *Guide to Federal Archives Relating to the Civil War. National Archives Publication No. 63-1.* Washington, D.C. Government Printing Office, 1962.

Carter, Fran. Searching American Military Records. Orting, WA: Heritage Quest, Inc.1991.

Coggins, J. *Arms and Equipment of the Civil War.* Garden City, New York: Doubleday & Company, 1962.

Dornbusch, Charles E. *Military Bibliography* of *the Civil War.* New York: The New York Public Library. Arno Press, Inc., 1961-62 Reprint. 1971.

Everton, G. *Handbook for Genealogists.* Logan, Utah: Everton Publishers, Inc., 2008.

Greenwood, Val D. *The Researcher's Guide to American Genealogy.* Baltimore, MD: Genealogical Publishing Co. Inc., 1990.

Groene, Bertram H. *Tracing Your Civil War Ancestor.* Winston-Salem, NC: John F. Blair, Publisher, 1973.

Massie, L. *Indian Tears and Petticoat Pioneers.* Allegan Forest, Michigan: Bookcrafters, 1994.

Military Service Records: A select Catalog of National Archives Microfilm Publications. Washington, D.C.: Government Printing Office, 1985.

Munden, Kenneth W. and Beers, Henry. P. *Guide to the Federal Archives Relating to the Civil War. National Archives Publication No.63-1.* Washington, D.C.: Government Printing Office, 1962.

Neagles, James C. *Confederate Research Sources.* Salt Lake City, UT: Ancestry, Inc., 1986.

Post, Gerald R. *The Civil War Diary and Biography of George W. Bailey.* Colleyville, TX: the author, 1991.

Schweitzer, George K. *Civil War Genealogy.* Knoxville, TN: the author, 1988.

Schweitzer, George K. *Handbook of Genealogical Sources.* Knoxville, TN: the author, 1996.

Smolenyak M. and Turner A. *Trace Your Roots with DNA.* Holtzbrinck Publishers, 2004

Soper, Stephen. *The 'Glorious Old Third': The History of the Third Michigan Infantry*, 1855-1927. steve@oldthirdmichigan.org: the author, 2006

White, Virgil. *Register of Florida CSA Pension Applications.* Waynesboro, TN: National Historical Publishing Co., 1989.

Wiltshire, Betty C. *Mississippi Confederate Pension Applications.* Carrollton, MS: Pioneer Publishing Co., 1994.

INDEX